AF588273

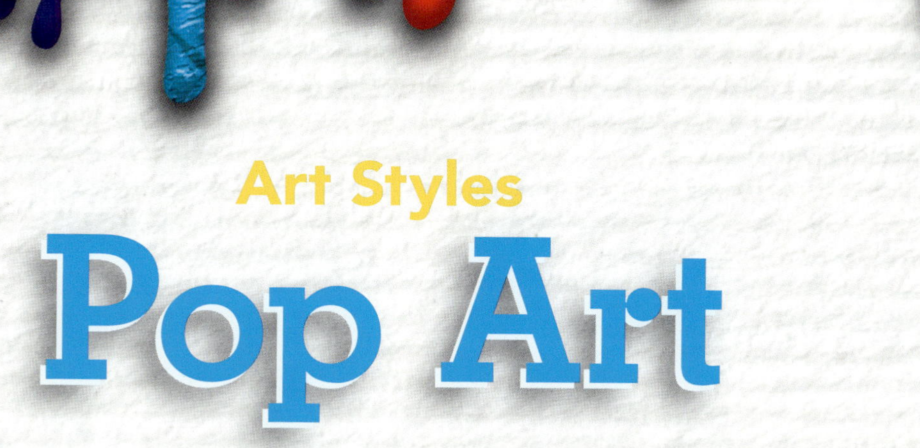

Art Styles

Pop Art

by Julie Murray

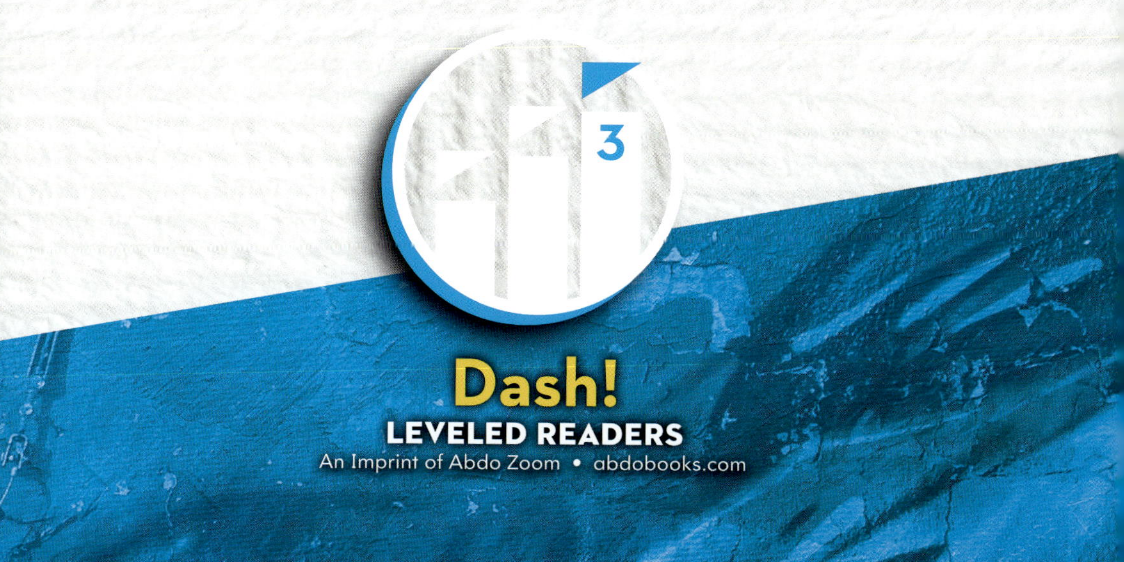

Dash!
LEVELED READERS
An Imprint of Abdo Zoom • abdobooks.com

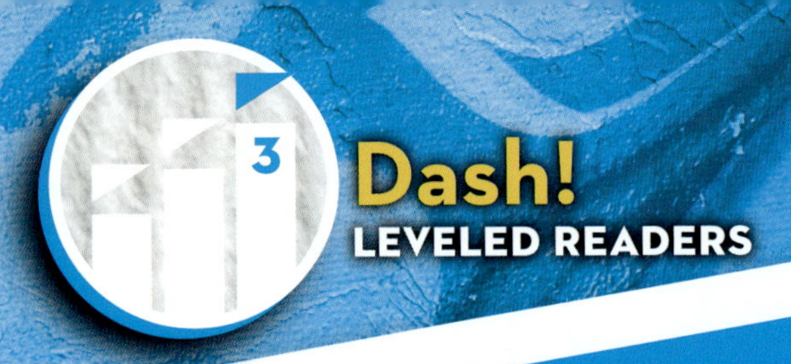

Level 1 – Beginning
Short and simple sentences with familiar words or patterns for children who are beginning to understand how letters and sounds go together.

Level 2 – Emerging
Longer words and sentences with more complex language patterns for readers who are practicing common words and letter sounds.

Level 3 – Transitional
More developed language and vocabulary for readers who are becoming more independent.

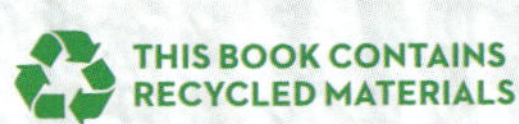

abdobooks.com

Published by Abdo Zoom, a division of ABDO, PO Box 398166, Minneapolis, Minnesota 55439.

Printed in the United States of America, North Mankato, Minnesota.
102023
012024

Photo Credits: Alamy, Getty Images, Shutterstock, ©The estate of Eduardo Paolozzi p7
Production Contributors: Kenny Abdo, Jennie Forsberg, Grace Hansen, John Hansen
Design Contributors: Candice Keimig, Neil Klinepier

Library of Congress Control Number: 2023937929

Publisher's Cataloging in Publication Data

Names: Murray, Julie, author.
Title: Pop art / by Julie Murray
Description: Minneapolis, Minnesota : Abdo Zoom, 2024 | Series: Art styles | Includes online resources and index.
Identifiers: ISBN 9781098283964 (lib. bdg.) | ISBN 9781098284688 (eBook) | ISBN 9781098285043 (Read-to-Me eBook)
Subjects: LCSH: Pop art--Juvenile literature. | New super-realism--Juvenile literature. | Neo-Dadaism--Juvenile literature. | Popular culture--Juvenile literature. | Art, Modern--Juvenile literature.
Classification: DDC 709.040--dc23

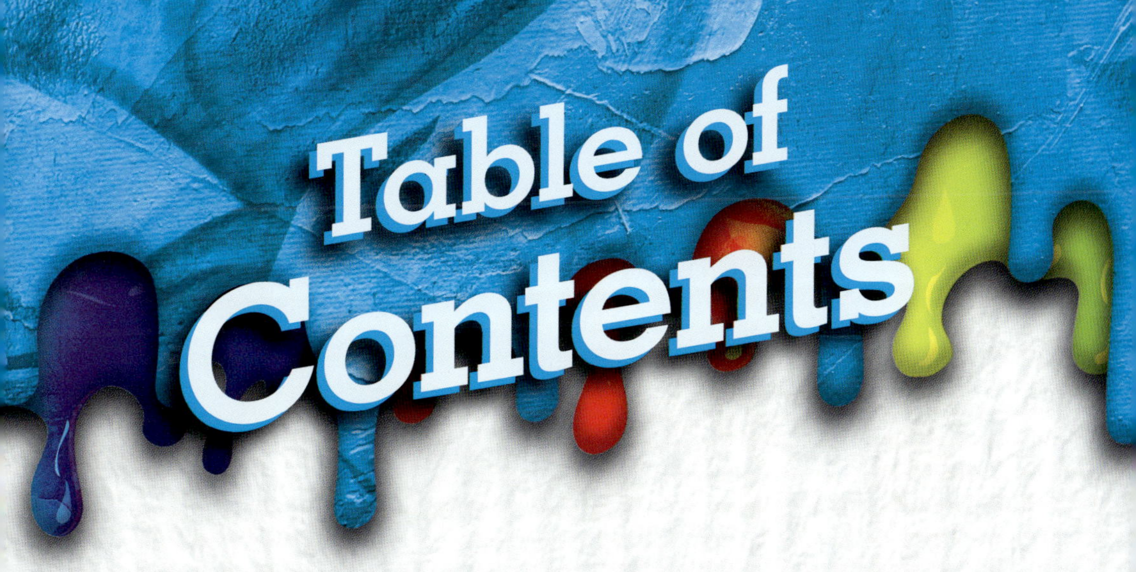

Table of Contents

Pop Art

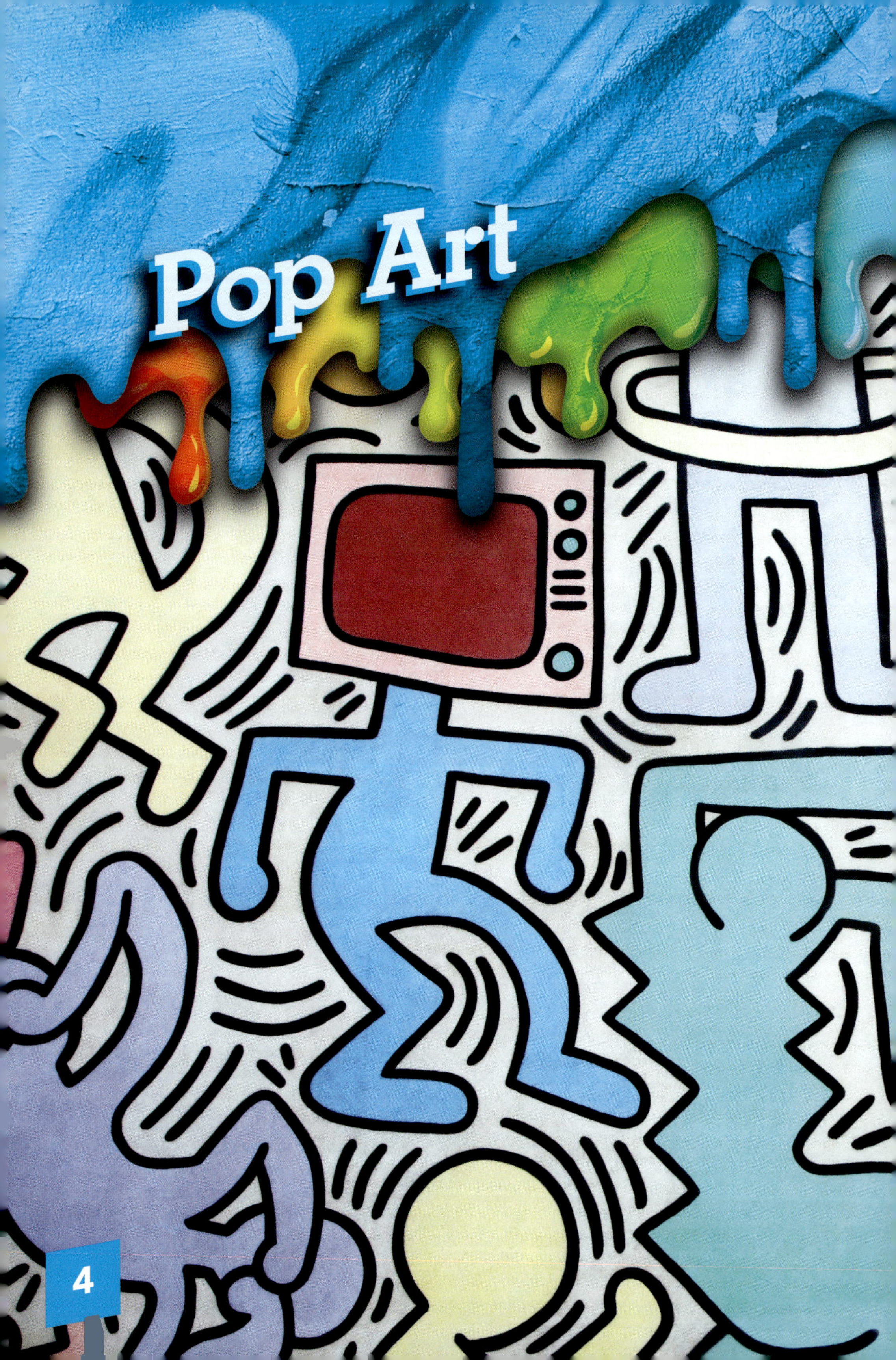

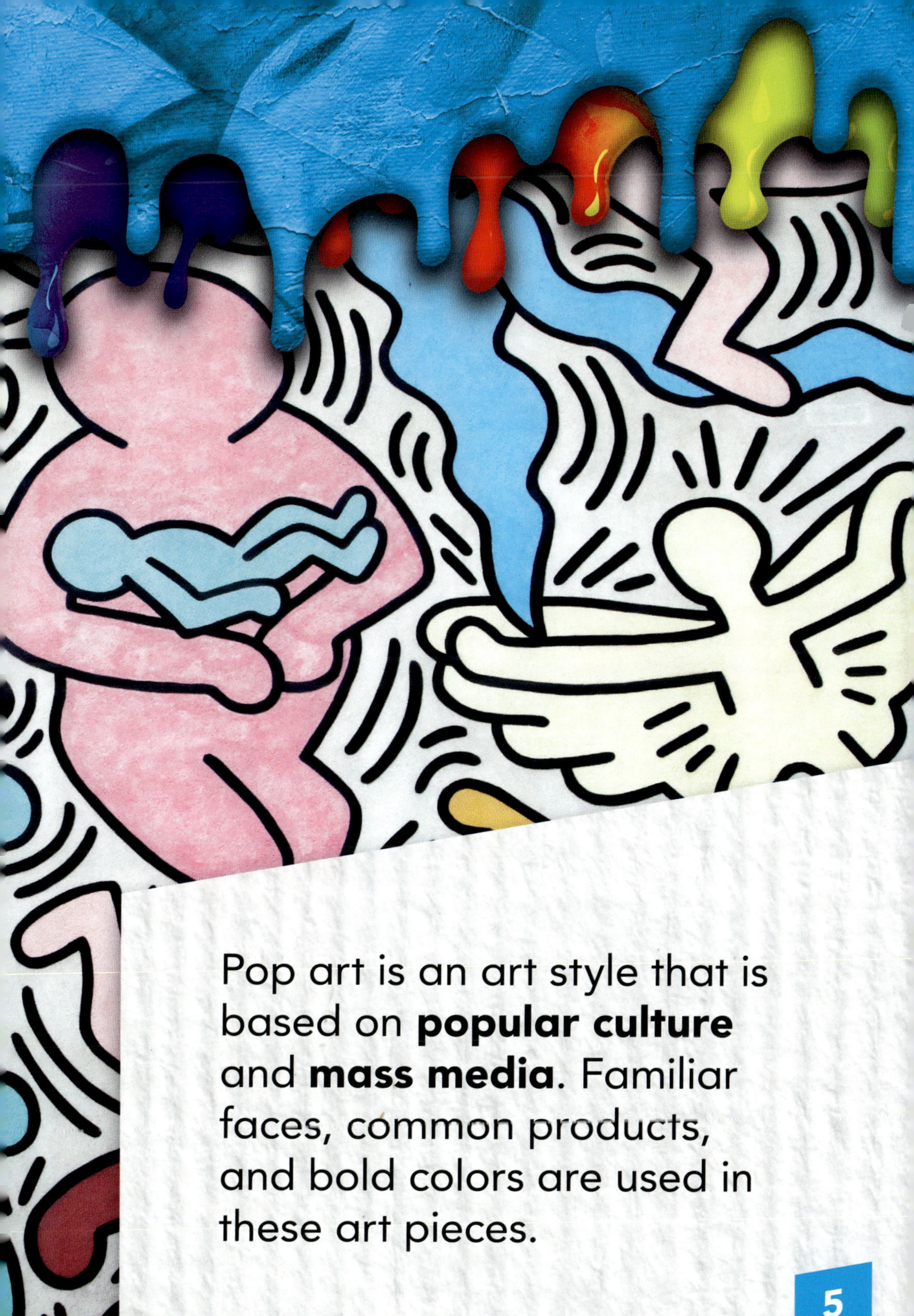

Pop art is an art style that is based on **popular culture** and **mass media**. Familiar faces, common products, and bold colors are used in these art pieces.

History

Pop art began in Great Britain in the early 1950s. Eduardo Paolozzi is one of the first Pop artists. His early collages were different and exciting.

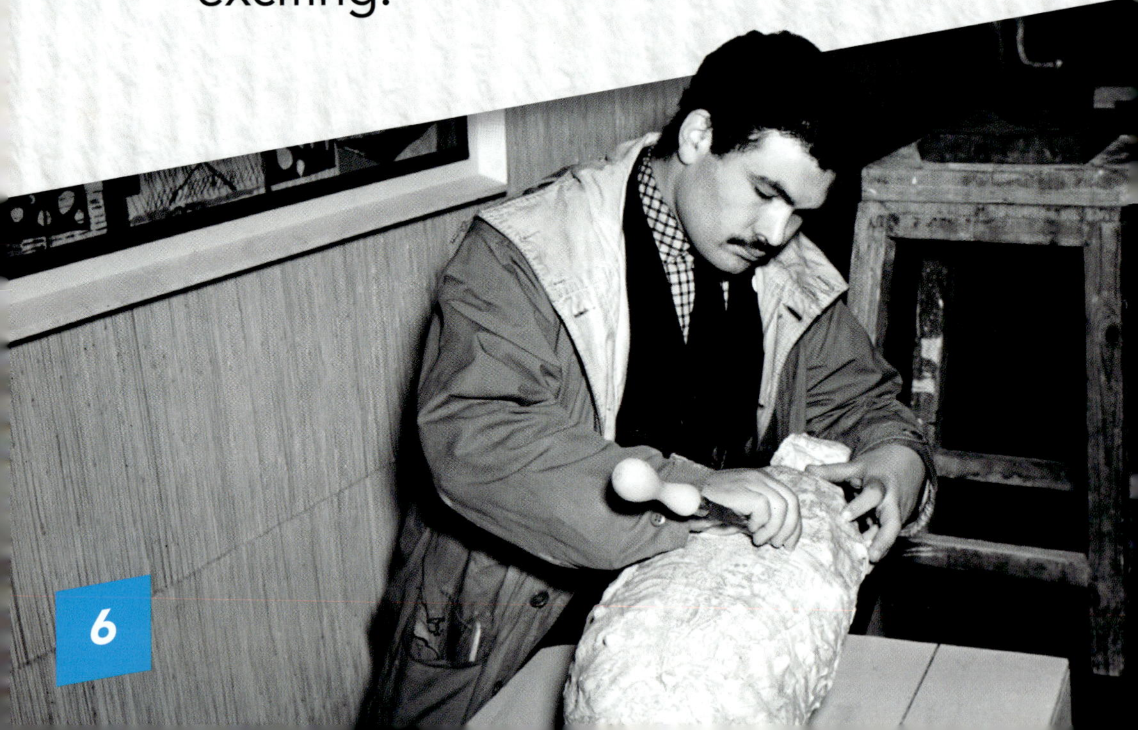

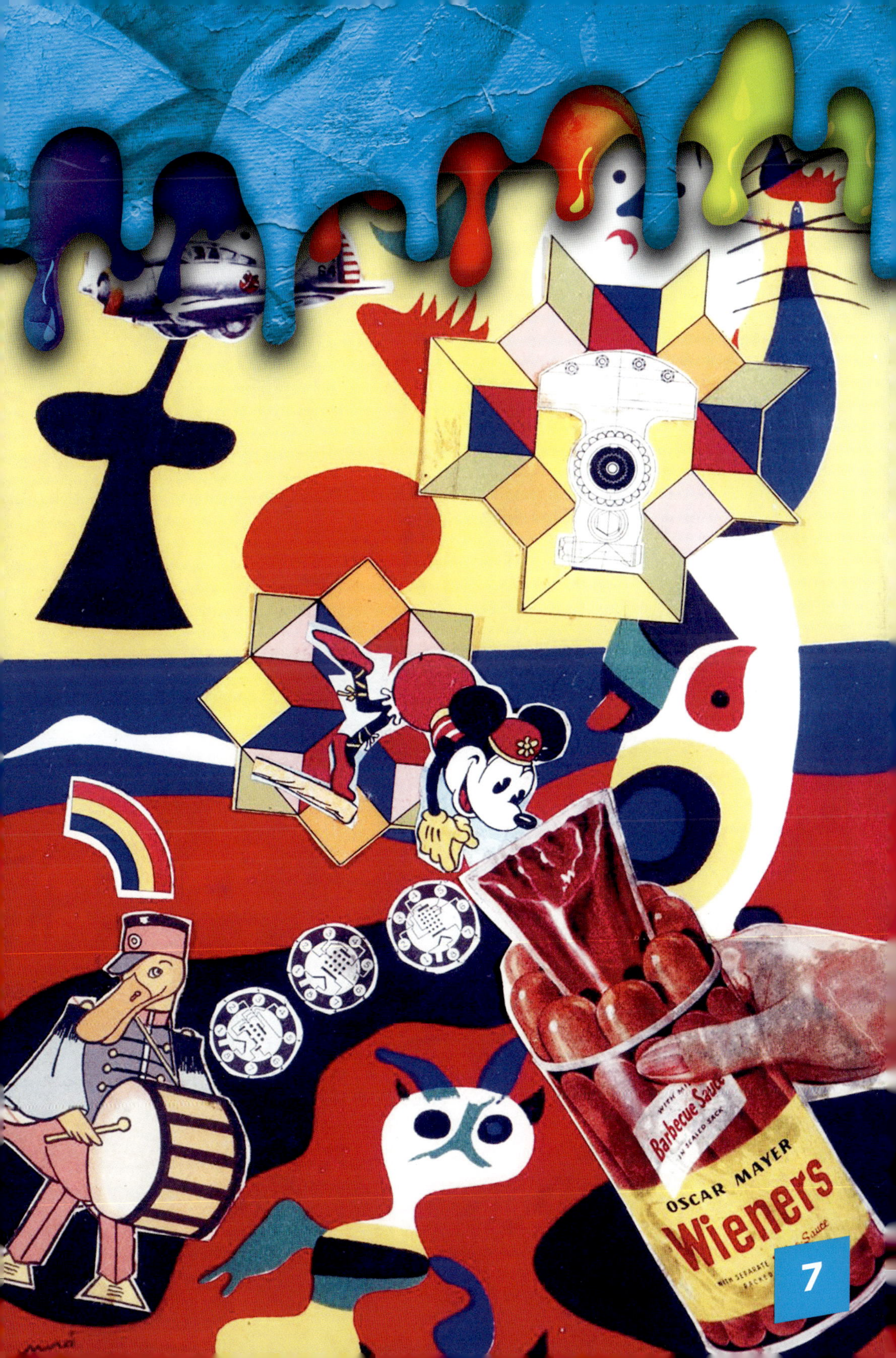
Barbecue Sauce
IN SEALED SACK
OSCAR MAYER
Wieners

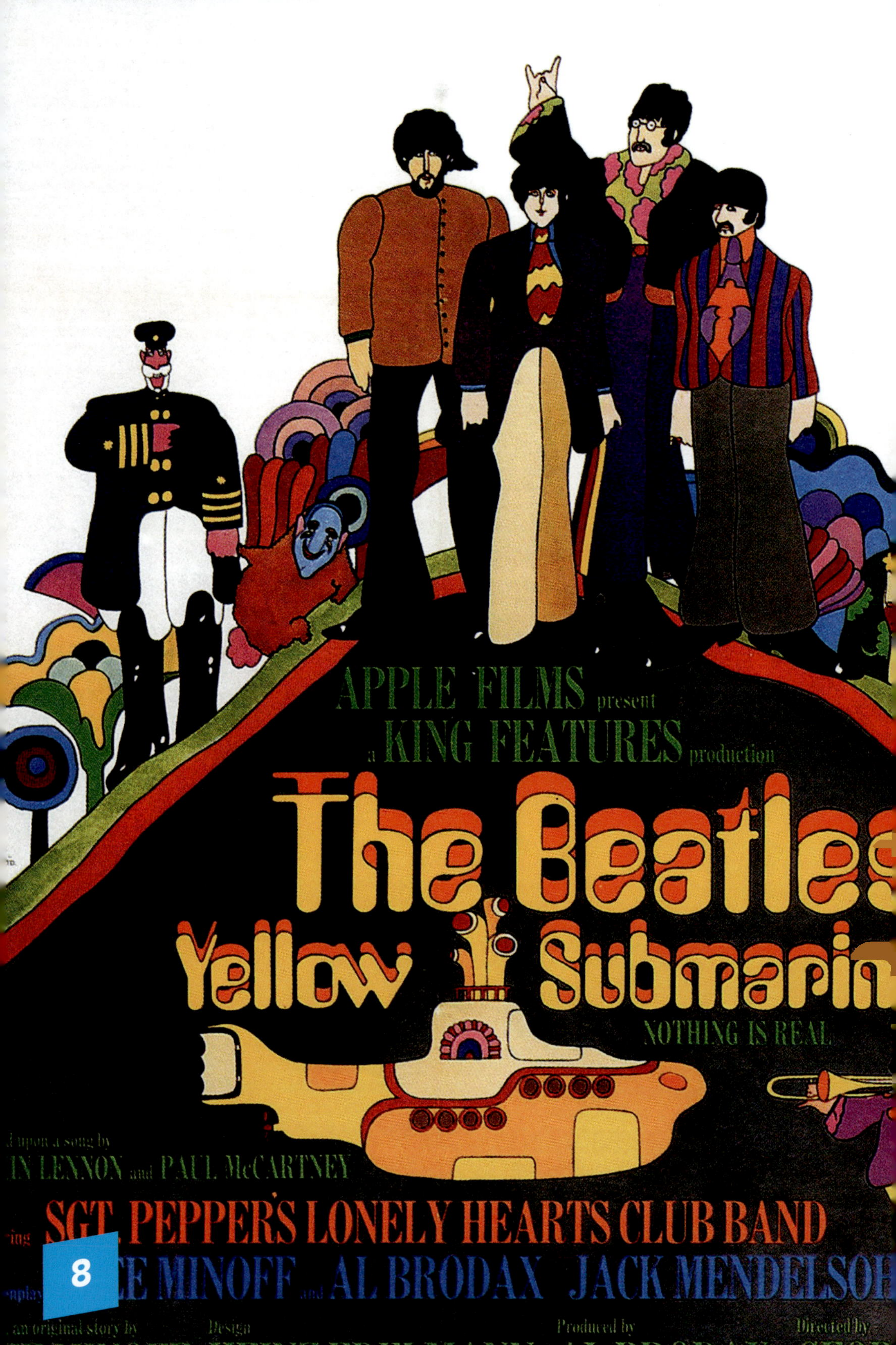
APPLE FILMS present
a KING FEATURES production
The Beatles
Yellow Submarin
NOTHING IS REAL
LENNON and PAUL McCARTNEY
SGT. PEPPER'S LONELY HEARTS CLUB BAND
MINOFF and AL BRODAX JACK
an original story by
Design
Produced by
Directed by

Pop art became popular in the United States in the early 1960s. Advertisements and comic strips played a big role in the Pop art movement coming to America.

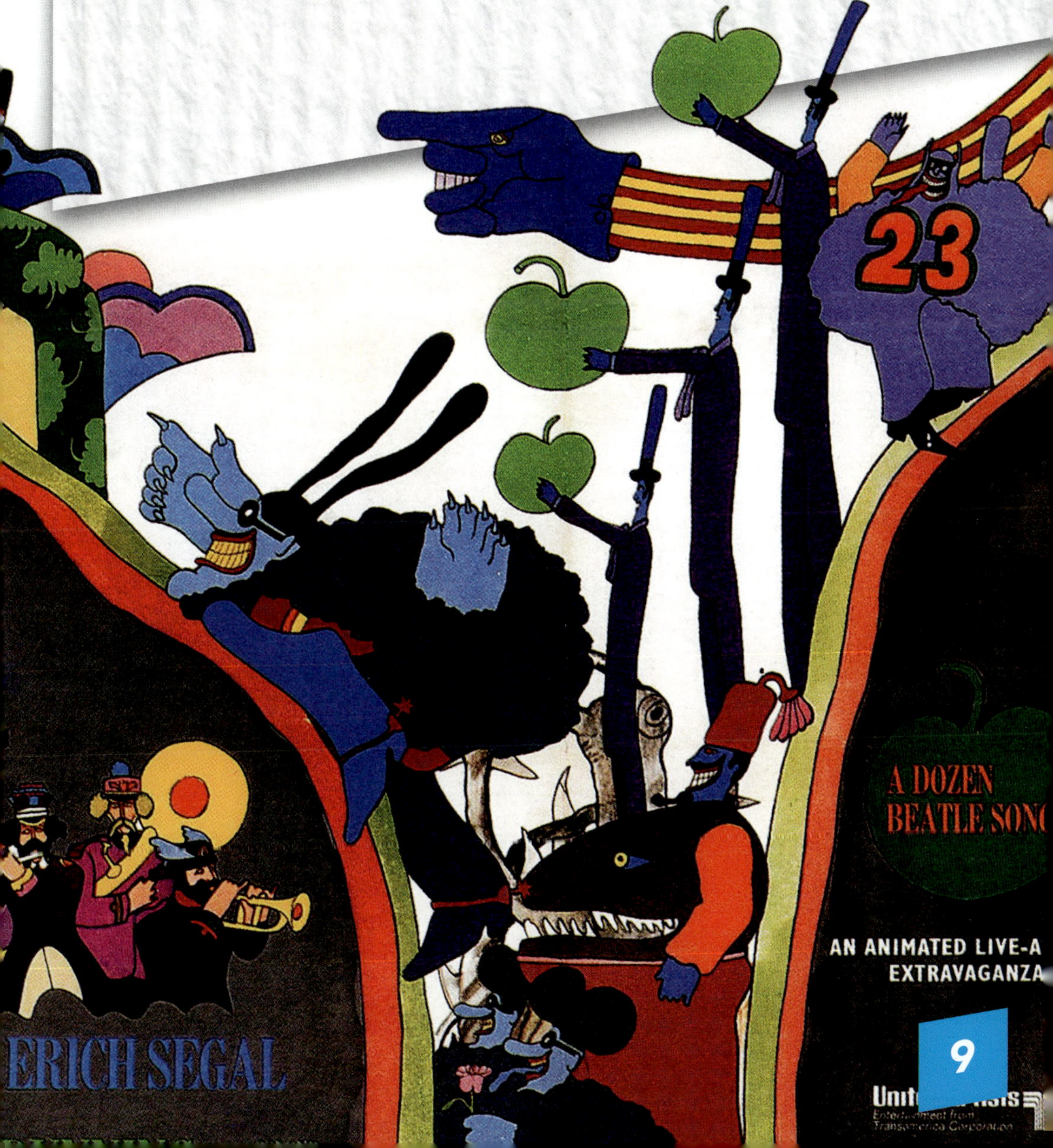

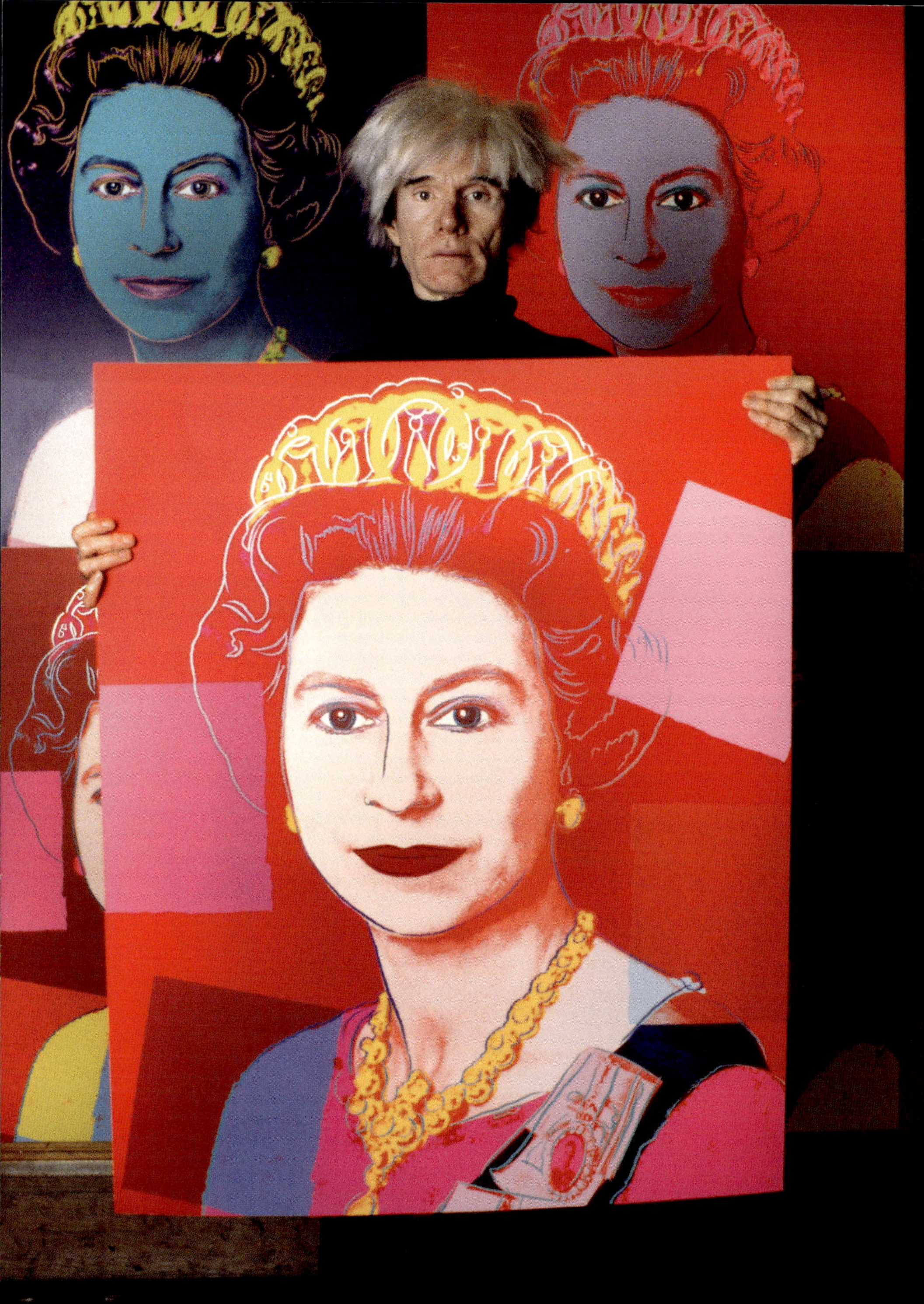

Andy Warhol is the most famous American Pop artist. He is known for his portraits of celebrities. He is also known for his prints of Campbell's soup cans and Coca-Cola bottles.

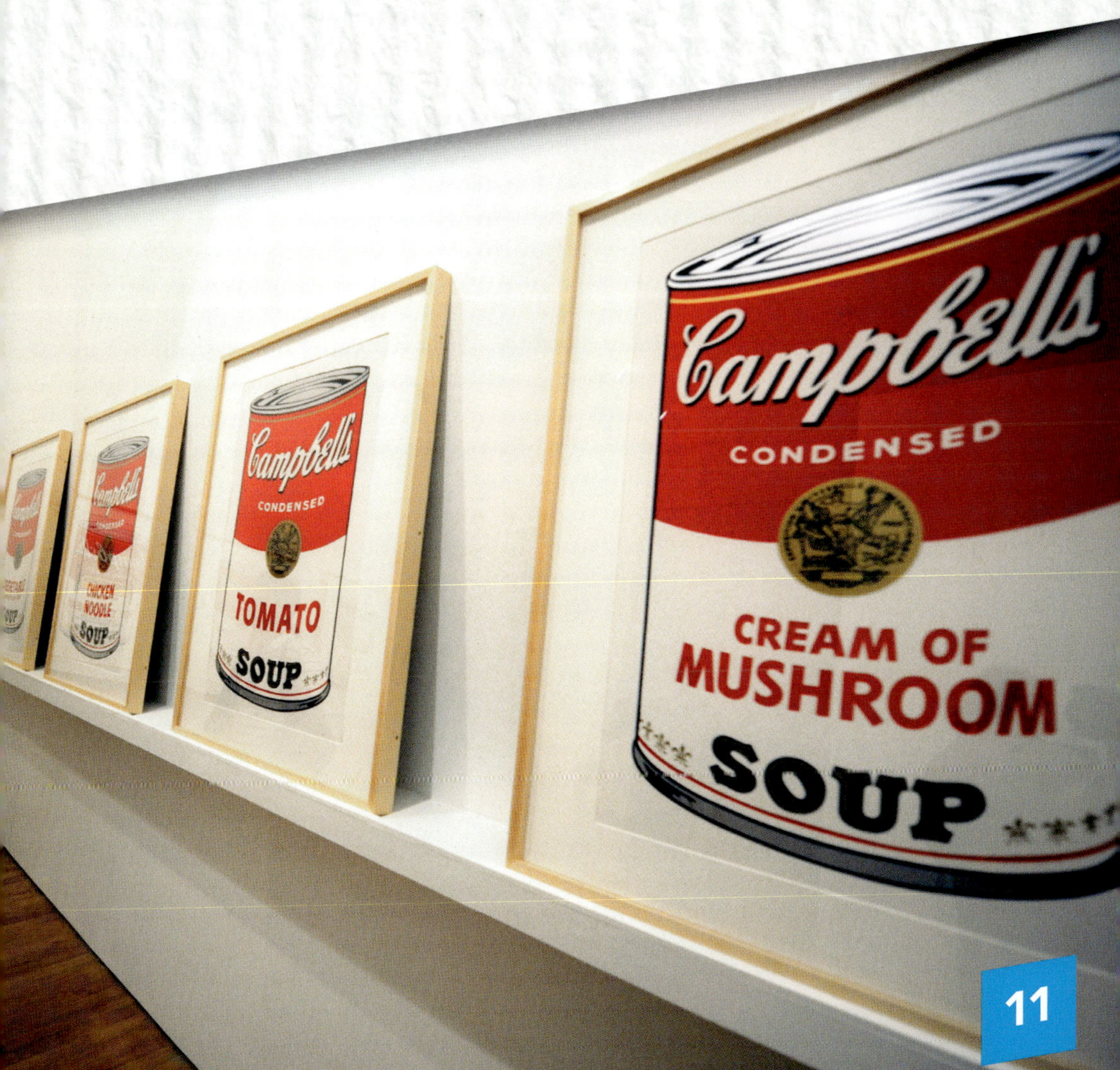

Pop art is also seen in other forms. The *LOVE* sculpture in New York City is a hit with tourists. The *Spoonbridge and Cherry* is an iconic piece in Minneapolis, Minnesota.

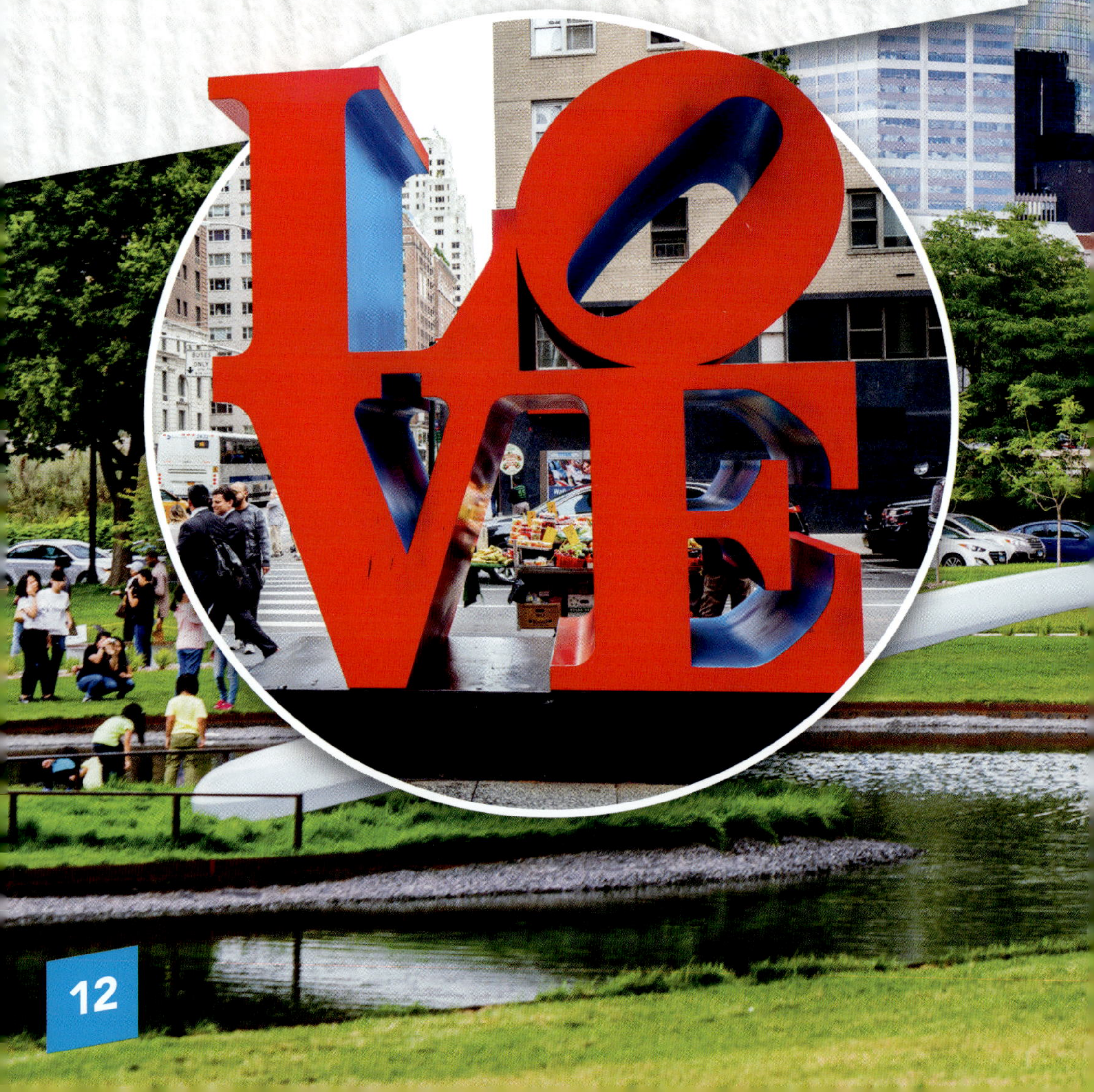

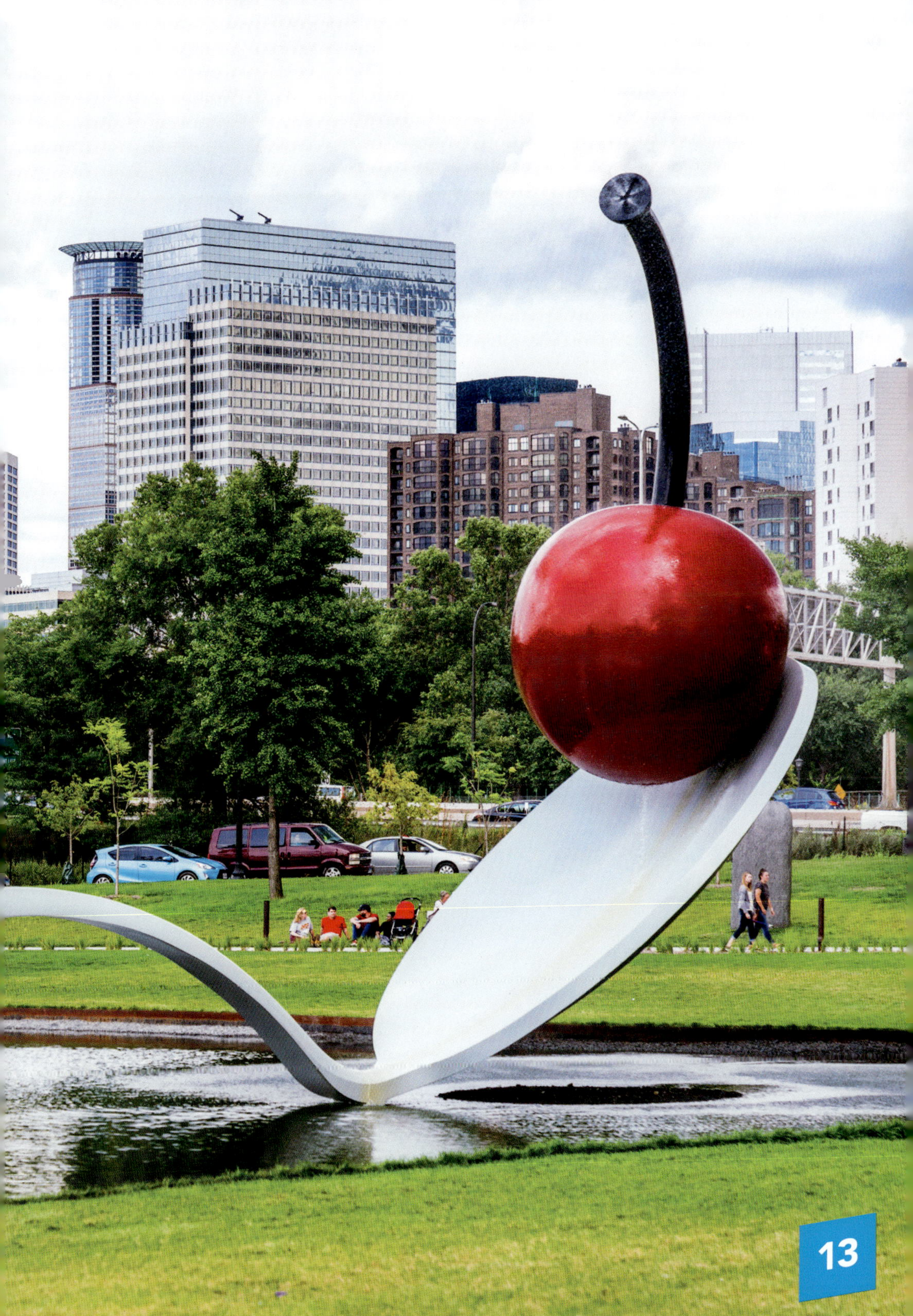

Characteristics of Pop Art

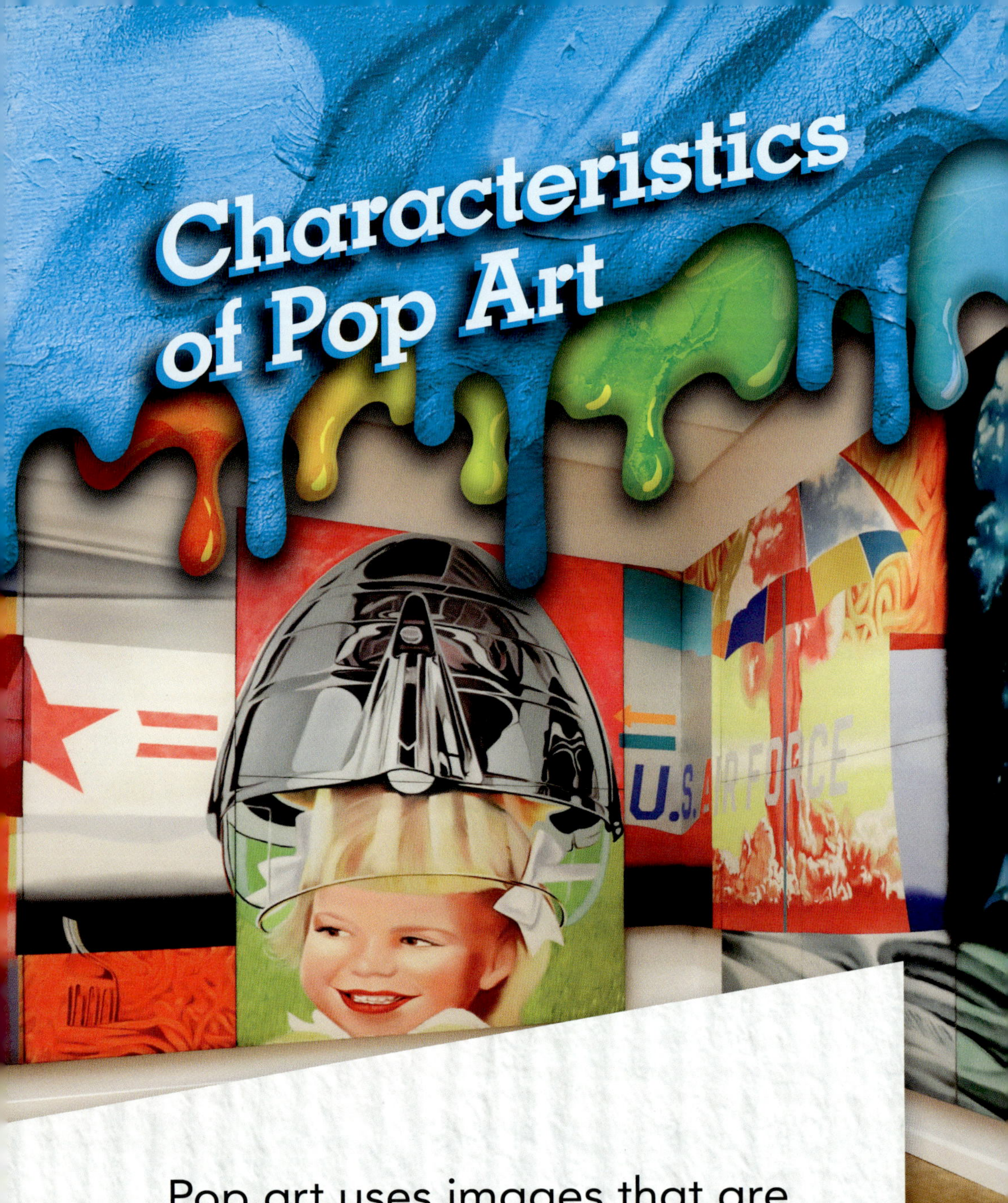

Pop art uses images that are popular and recognizable. Everyday objects are often the subject of the art pieces.

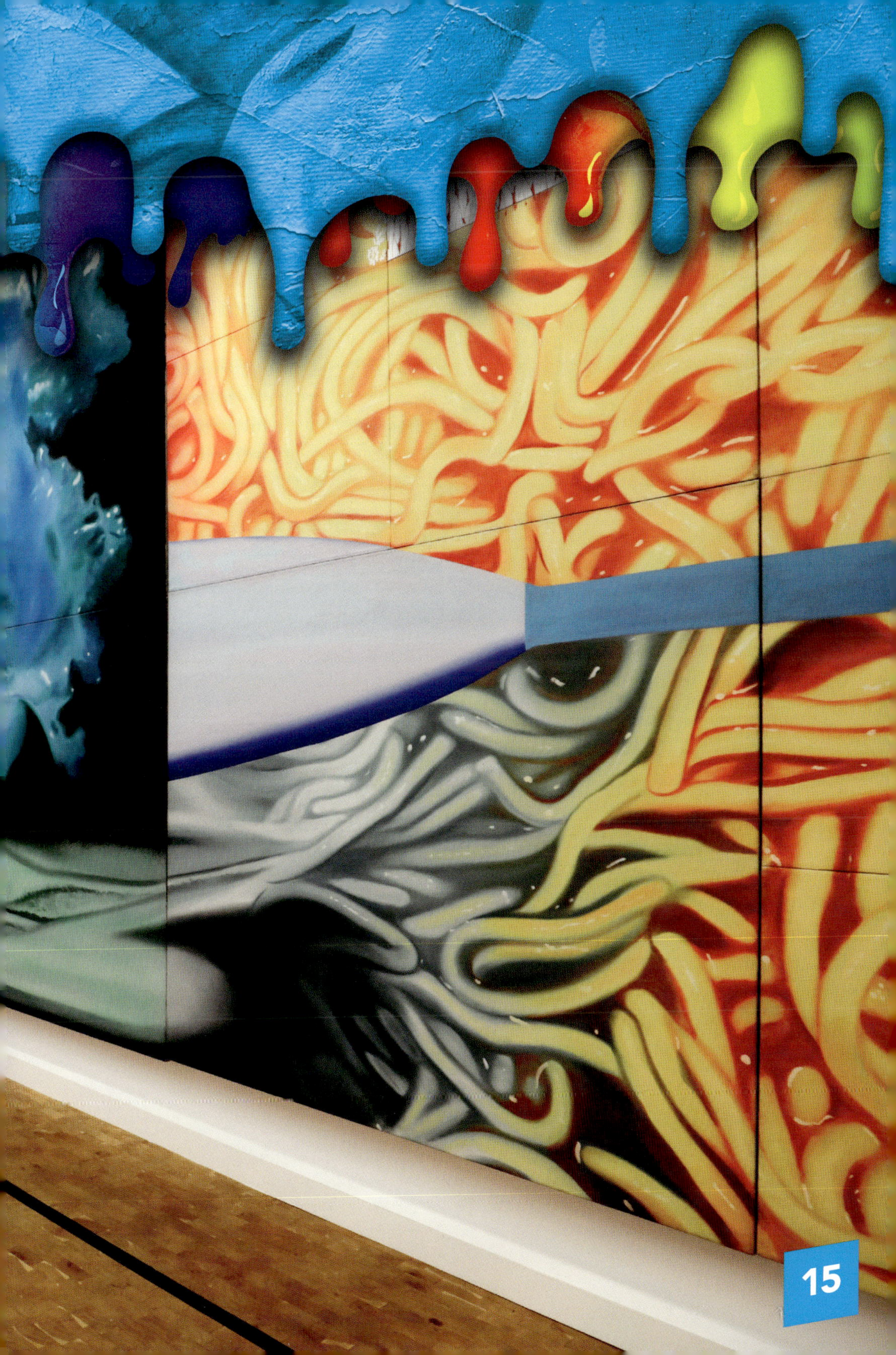

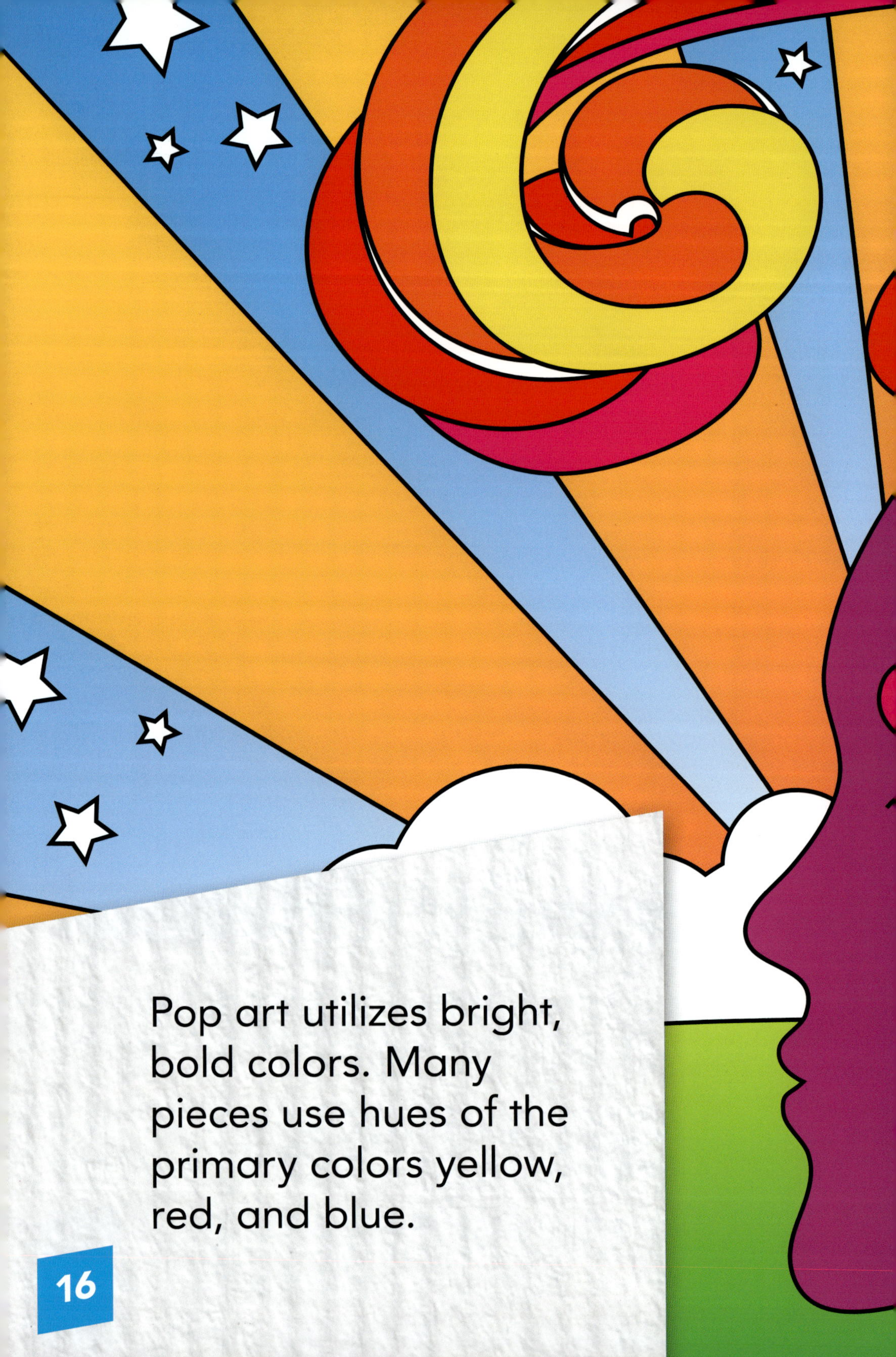

Pop art utilizes bright, bold colors. Many pieces use hues of the primary colors yellow, red, and blue.

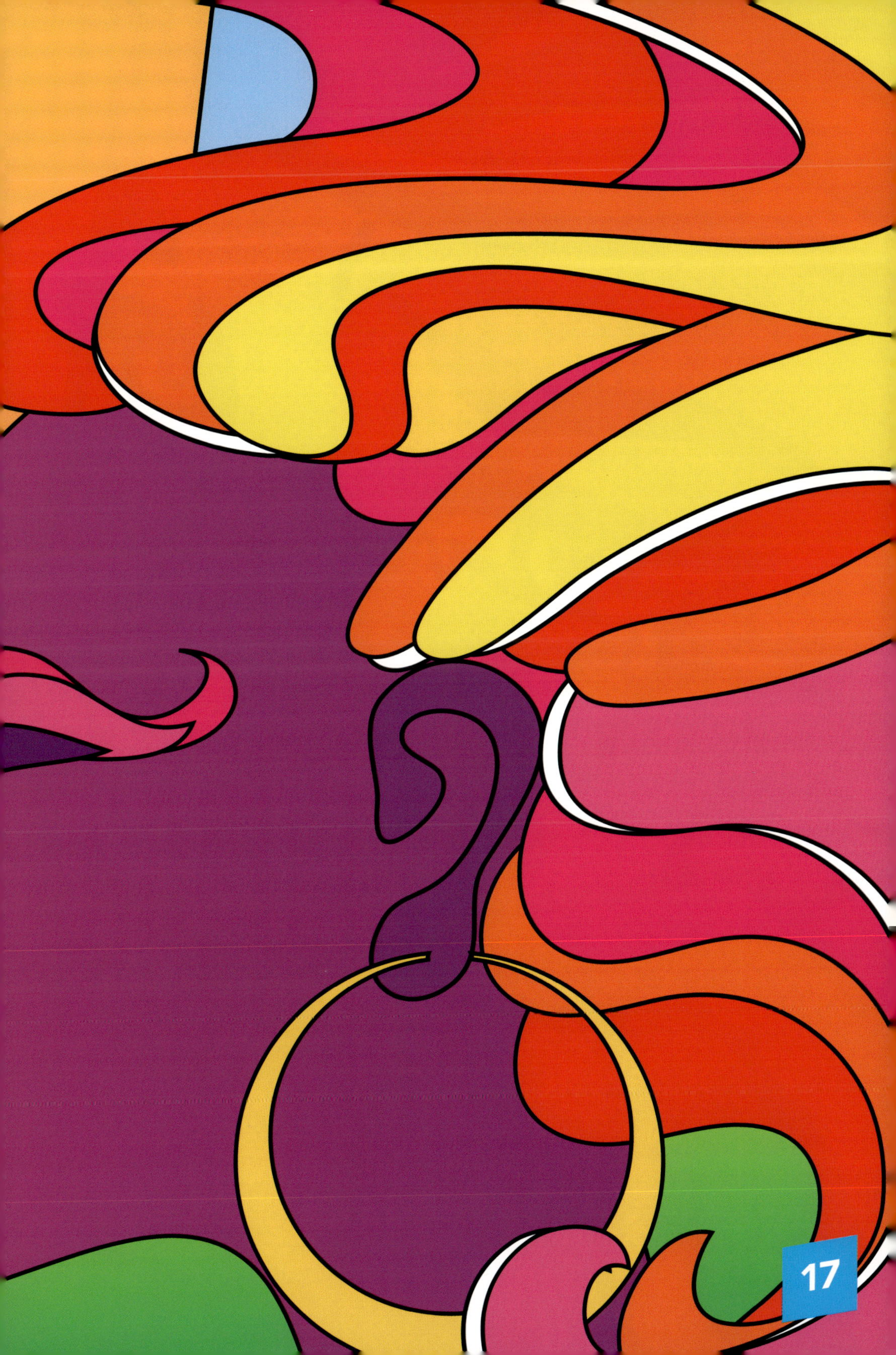

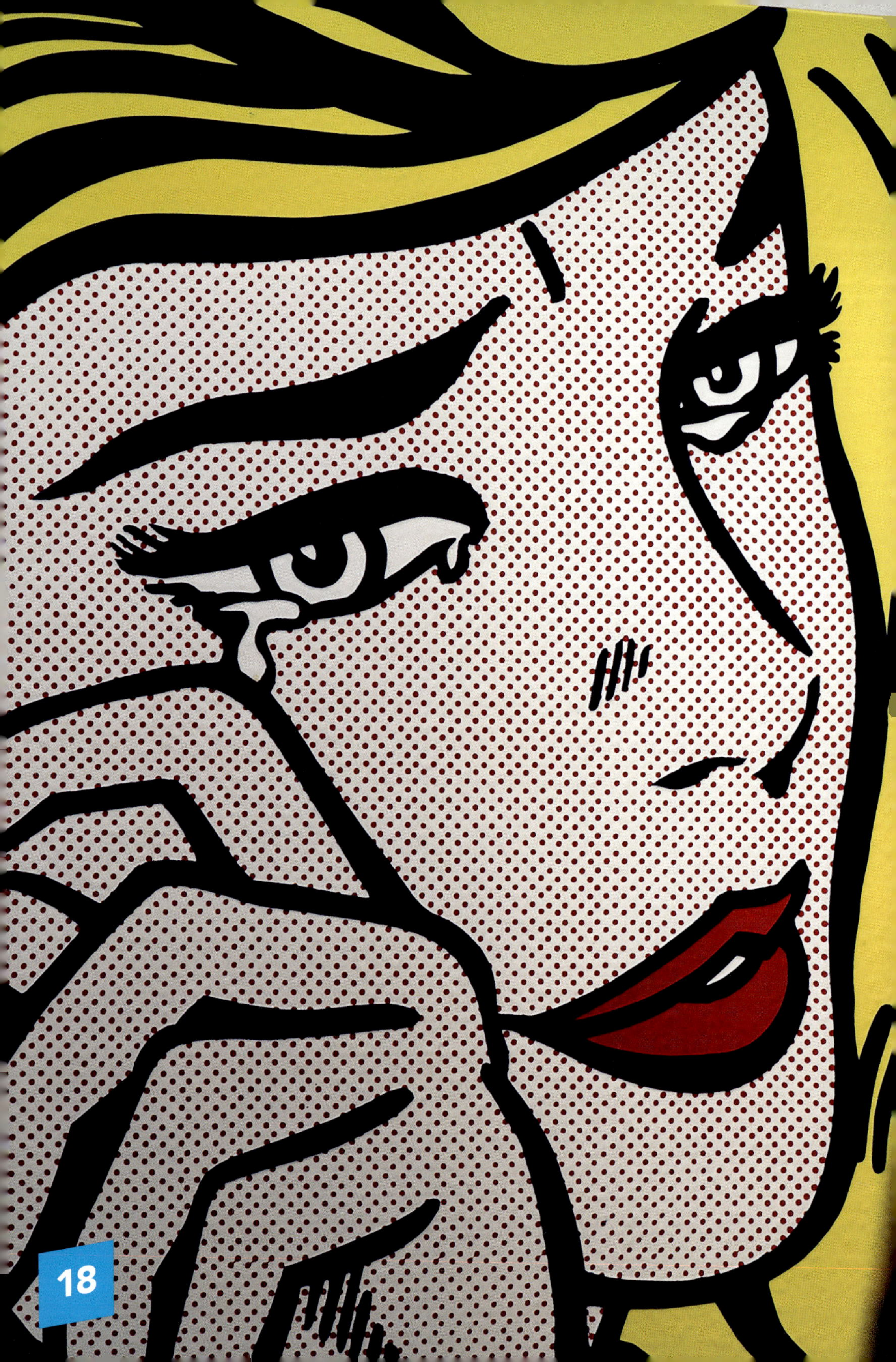

Pop art is created using many different techniques, such as media and screen printing. Roy Lichtenstein used **Ben-Day dots** to create many of his art pieces.

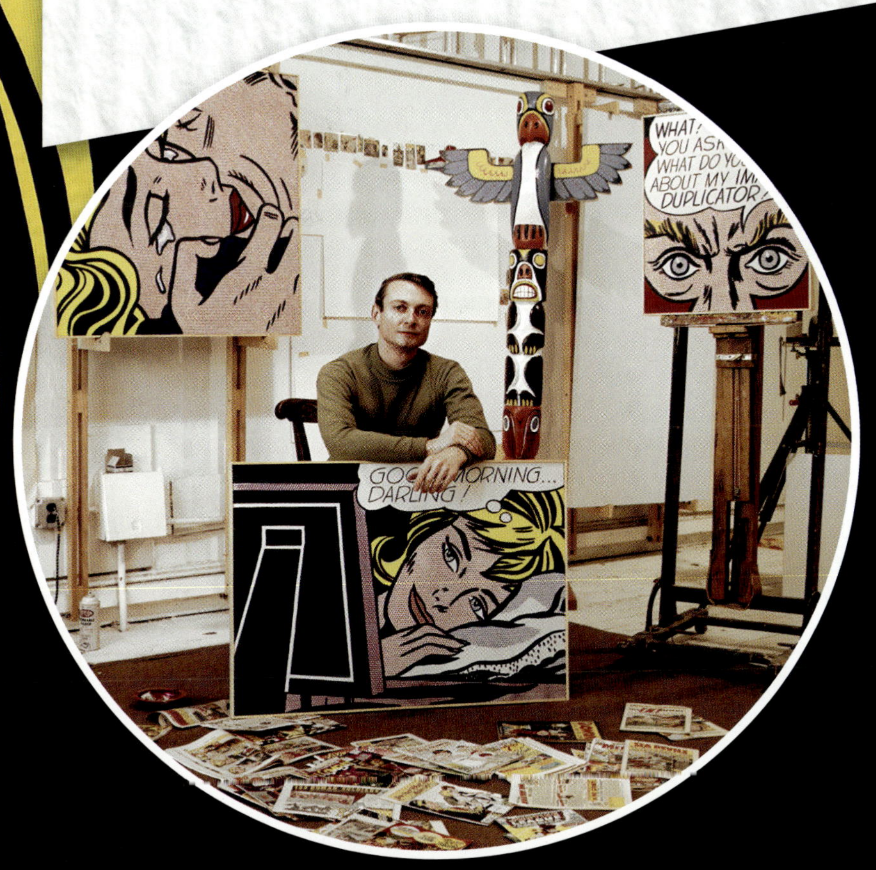

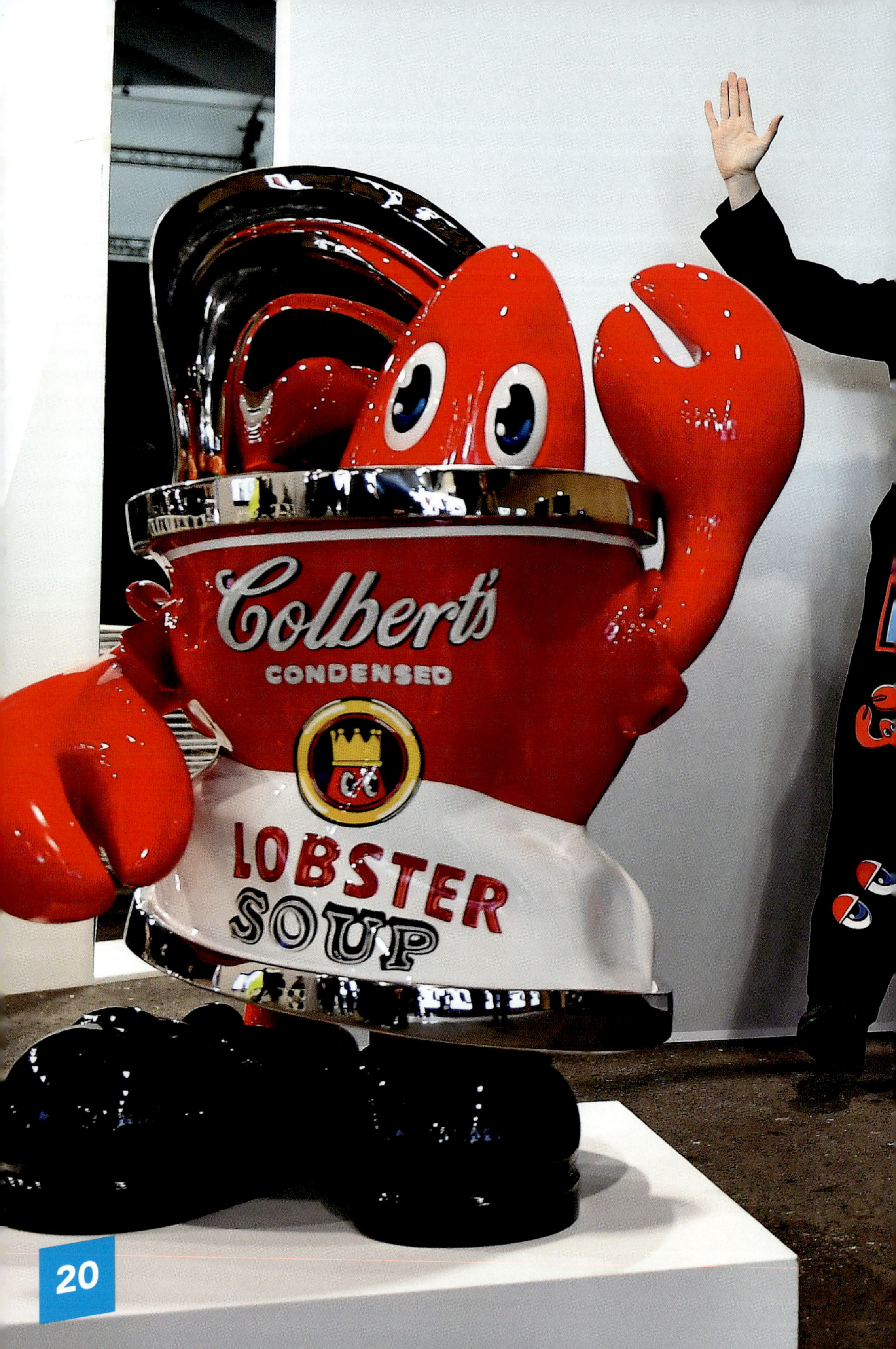
Colbert's
CONDENSED
LOBSTER
SOUP

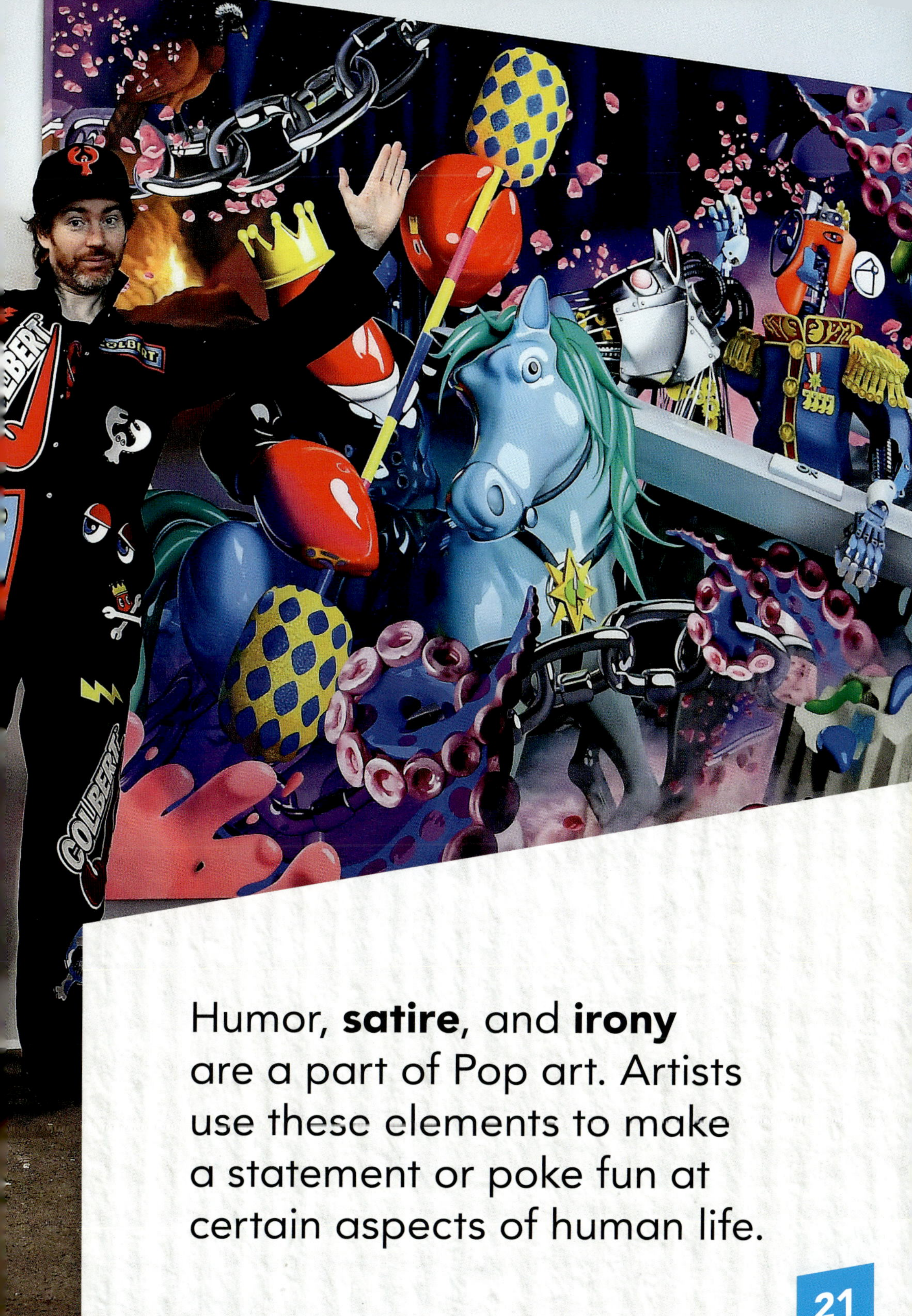

Humor, **satire**, and **irony** are a part of Pop art. Artists use these elements to make a statement or poke fun at certain aspects of human life.

More Facts

- Pop art was sometimes called "anti-art." It was seen as a rebellion against traditional art styles.
- Pop art played a significant role in opening up art to the general public. Before this, many thought that art was only for high society.
- In 1962, Andy Warhol sold 32 Campbell's soup can paintings for $1,000. In 1996, they were valued at $15 million!

Glossary

Ben-Day dots – an inexpensive mechanical printing method which relies upon small colored dots that are variously spaced and combined to create shading and colors in images.

irony – contrast that is usually interesting or surprising between what one would normally expect and what the real thing or situation is.

mass media – those ways of communicating that reach large numbers of people, such as magazines and television.

popular culture – the part of culture, especially the arts, that appeals to or is consumed by the masses.

satire – the use of humor, irony, or exaggeration to expose people's stupidity or vices.

Index

Online Resources

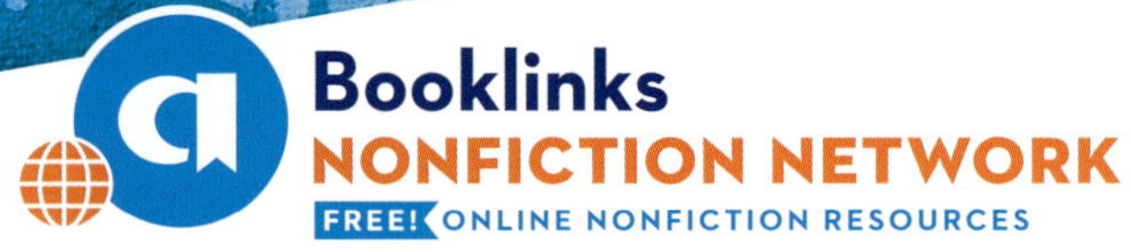

To learn more about Pop art, please visit **abdobooklinks.com** or scan this QR code. These links are routinely monitored and updated to provide the most current information available.